Trouble

Poems, Including "Hannah Alive"
by Anne Harding Woodworth

Trouble

Poems, Including "Hannah Alive"
by Anne Harding Woodworth

Turning Point

© 2020 by Anne Harding Woodworth

Published by Turning Point
P.O. Box 541106
Cincinnati, OH 45254-1106

ISBN: 9781625493613

Poetry Editor: Kevin Walzer
Business Editor: Lori Jareo

Visit us on the web at www.turningpointbooks.com

Poetry by Anne Harding Woodworth

Books
The Eyes Have It
Unattached Male
The Artemis Sonnets, Etc.
Spare Parts: A Novella in Verse
The Mushroom Papers
Guide to Greece and Back

Chapbooks
The Last Gun
Herding
Up from the Root Cellar
Aesop's Eagles

for Leda, Nico, Henry, Jonathan, Sophie, Annabel, and Steve

The husband mentioned a particular poet who's having great success these days, then added, *but she's troubled.*

All the good poets are troubled, the wife said.
That's why I'm not a good poet.

To which the husband quickly replied, *Oh, but you <u>are</u> troubled, honey.*

Acknowledgments

"Amuse Bouche, the Ortolan" in *Crannog*, No. 40, Autumn 2015

"Artist's Blue Hour," in *Anthology of Featured Poets*, Moonstone Poetry Series, Philadelphia: The Moonstone Press, 2015

"Birds Keep No Borders," in *The Skinny Poetry Anthology*, ed. Truth Thomas, Cherry Castle Publishing, 2019

"Ella at the Turn of the Century," in slightly different form, *Sunlight on the Moon*, Barbara de la Cuesta and Nancy Dowd, eds. Island Heights, NJ: Carpenter Gothic Publishing, 1998

"Good-Luck Bin," online at https://thewriterscafemagazine.wordpress.com/2018/04/16/the-writers-cafe-magazine-issue-7-shoes/

"Hannah Alive," nos. 2, 4, 16, 23, 24, 26, 27 in *Poetry Salzburg Review*, No. 28, Autumn 2015; no. 5 as "Hannah Remembers the Rosenbergs" in *Strange Fruit: Poems on the Death Penalty,* Sarah Zale and Terry Persun, eds., Wildflower Press, 2019; no. 19 as "Hannah as Accomplice" in *Adana,* Diane Lockward and Lynne McEniry, eds., 2014

"Horse Dress," online in *Melancholy Hyperbole* https://melancholyhyperbole.com/2014/07/19/horse-dress-1939/

"I Am Not Joan Rivers" online in *Antiphon*, Issue 17 http://antiphon.org.uk/wordpress/wp-content/uploads/2016/02/Antiphon-issue-17.pdf

"Jealousy," in *Connoisseurs of Suffering,* Jason Dias and Louis Hoffman, University Professors Press, 2017, p. 95

"Kingdom of Blood" in *Bared: Contemporary Poetry and Art on Bras and Breasts*, Les Femmes Folles Books, 2017

"The Miniaturist,1828" in *Ekphrasis*, 2016

"On Seeing *Psycho* in a Concert Hall," in *Little Patuxent Review*, Issue 14, Summer 2013; also online at *Verse Daily*, http://www.versedaily.org/2014/psychoconcert.shtml

"Over-Abundance" appeared on *Poetry X Hunger*'s website (PoetryXHunger.com) and Facebook page for winning Third Prize in the 2019 World Food Day Poetry Competition sponsored by the United Nations' Food and Agriculture Organization.

"Quiet Air" in *Poem, Revised*, Robert Hartwell Fiske and Laura Cherry, eds., Oak Park IL: Marion Street Press, 2008

"Stuart Among the Nightingales," online in *Referential Magazine,* December 2013

"Walt's Notebook," online at *Beltway Poetry Quarterly*, issue 18:1, Winter 2017 http://www.beltwaypoetry.com/walts-notebook/; and in *Endlessly Rocking*, Stan Galloway and Nicole Yurcaba, eds., Englewood, NJ: Unbound Content, 2019

Table of Contents

1 Hannah Alive

Death is a time for solitude.—Hannah Hyatt O'Reilly

Hannah Alive

1

In my 80s, I'm remembering when I was five.
I knew one fact about a kid named Peter—
he was the son of a man found
hanging in a closet.

My father dressed in a closet.
His closet had a window
and sometimes I'd watch him
looking out into the orchard.

What did he see in the orchard
where I played every day?
Fathers don't see everything.
They stare into spaces we don't see.

2

I look out the windows
here in my apartment.
It's what I do now,
besides taking Max for walks
and swimming in the city pool,
which I can do again
now that the pandemic is over.
Water is my cleanser,
Max my sounding board.

3

I was seven and saw
my great-grandfather
in a nursing home
before he died.
It was easy
to consider him dead.
He appeared dead
still breathing.
I looked for movement
under the sheet.
No one showed surprise
when he became dead,
but they still held a mirror
under his nose.

4

I didn't know my grandmother.
She died on my second birthday.
Without lingering, as they put it.
That was her good fortune—
and her heirs'—to exit early,
to avoid prolonging what they call now
with bowed heads "end of life."

One day, alive. Next, lying on an undertaker's slab.

And me, cheated of a grandmother.
People used to tell me
you could make anything happen
if you wanted it enough. Max does.
So, I prayed my grandmother would come back.
In the bathtub. I prayed in the tub.

Water has always soothed me.
I'm not sure what I prayed to.
Praying's never been
much of a successful activity for me,

though I did get baptized, which I've always hoped
would do me some good someday.
If you don't have a religion—and I don't—
there's always that gnat in the back of your mind
that maybe you're wrong, an idea that gets
intense at my age. I feel lucky to have
that baptism in my back pocket.

5

Besides Peter's father's hanging,
the Rosenbergs' death has stayed with me.

It's grown with me. I was a teenager
when it happened. The chair they ended up in,

one after the other, was square and woody,
almost Mission-style like some we used to have.

Oak, but theirs was strewn with wires
that zapped the body.

The electric chair and the Rosenbergs in it
made me think about death, and my fingers

tingled with fear. But back then I had nowhere to turn.
It was as if everyone around me wanted that couple to die.

They had two boys. Robert, Michael. I saw pictures of them
in magazines and made them my brothers.

I thought I could stop the execution of our parents—
kids feel responsible when parents go wrong.

A whole country let those parents sizzle.
A whole country lets others sizzle still

but more quietly now and—isn't it an irony?—
on a hospital gurney.

Up to the night the Rosenbergs died, I understood
nothing of electricity, animal or human.

Sure, I loved toast with butter and sourwood honey.
I loved my clock-radio and Your Hit Parade.

But that night, at 13, I learned how quick,
how candescent, how hot and treacherous

electricity could be, when switches are switched
and human beings twitch until dead.

6

At 15, I met Tony, a boy of 20,
college boy, frat boy, vodka boy.

He said, *drink. Vodka leaves
nothing on the breath.*

So we drank each other ever after,
slept each other, rubbed each other,

and gave each other babies
drinking vodka every evening

in a cocoon-household, trying to get through
a day-to-day routine of marriage, chicken nuggets,

jobs, jeans, roof, lawn mower, TV.
In those days, people had two children.

That was it. Zero Population Growth, they called it.
ZPG. Tony and I replaced ourselves with two boys.

It made a lot of sense. Still does to me,
but others don't see it that way anymore.

Families are getting big again—
the way skirts and dresses have come back.

7

Do young women today know how hard it was
to be allowed to wear trousers in the office back in the '70s?
Once again, women have to be careful
how they sit, what they wear underneath,
and their mobility is in jeopardy.

Same thing with stiletto heels. They're back in force,
slowing women up, making them waddle. It's quite funny
to watch them, especially when they're walking with men
who not so secretly enjoy winning the race. Women worked hard
to be heard, to get jobs, to get as close to equal pay as possible.

Equal pay won't happen in my lifetime,
not in skirts and high-heels.

8

But back to zero population.
There are just too many of us in the world today.
Too many people, in spite of scourges
like earthquakes, ebola, HIV, tsunamis, COVID-19,
tornadoes, and wars, endless wars,
hatred, killing human beings because of the way
they think, pray, look, or talk—
and of course guns, which are just
another branch of war.
If each one of us replaced our own self,
we'd keep things pretty steady.

And steady's good. Steady relieves
the mind. Steady opens eyes.
Steady quells jealousies. Steady
makes room for peace.

9

When I had my second boy,
a friend said, *poor Hannah.*
She'll have to try again.

As if getting a girl
was of any importance to me,
was going to make me whole.
Of course, in those days
we never knew what we were getting
until we were lying there spread-eagle
on the delivery table and pushing.
Truth is, I wanted a second boy.
I never said so, in case I got a girl.
But I knew the kind of girl I'd been.
A brooder. And later a rebel.
I made life miserable for my parents,
especially my mother.
I didn't want a daughter to do that to me.

10

When my second boy was in first grade,
I felt I deserved a return to myself. For me,
that meant the Guild, where I could sculpt
my clay figures, my stick people. I call them my sticks.

At the Guild I could pull my sticks into being,
fire them in a kiln, glaze them, display them, sell them.
Yet there it was— what they used to call
"a bun in the oven." And I speak with love.

I had no cravings this time, no roe v. caviar,
or pickles and ice cream. No, no cravings
other than to lose it. And the law made things
finally possible to lose it to a real doctor.

Afterward, my father accused me of murder.
But murder would cause nightmares, and I had none.
Men shouldn't pass judgment on us women.
They have so little understanding outside of themselves.

My mother never said a word. Women know what it is
to feel trapped. An older Greek woman once told me
she'd found herself pregnant during Nazi occupation
of Athens, when there was starvation everywhere.

She knew she couldn't bring a child into such a world.
And despite being sure she'd done the right thing,
she suffered ever afterward. Whereas, me, I didn't suffer.
I knew I had saved my family and my own life.

No phantom-child ever spoke to me in my dreams
or caused me to sink into an abyss. I spent more and more time
at the Guild making sticks. Yes, sometimes I wondered
how old? what grade? how tall? how happy? what color hair?

But did I murder it, something so tiny, so imprisoned
in my body through no will of its own, something so powerless
to live on the outside, to be a member of society?
Was I even capable of killing?

11

I got my own show at the Guild
to exhibit my sticks, my skinny leggy figures.
They called me a visionary artist,

because I was untaught except
by studying Leonard Baskin. His Dead Men.
His birds. His drawings of mortality. His owl.

Carroly Erickson says: "The visionary is a person
who sees what isn't there. . . .
In the middle ages, visions defined reality."

My sticks defined my reality, more than a child
ever should. Your sticks, Tony used to say, kill me.
And he'd shake his head laughing.

Really, he was competing with my sticks.
Sometimes I'd see him put his hand on one,
contemplate it as if he were Aristotle looking at Homer.

But I saw in his eyes a desire to pick it up
and *hurl* it across the room.
I placed my sticks all over the house we lived in then—

on shelves with the china, in bookcases, on end tables—
and I moved them around from room to room
each new stick—thinner than the one I'd made before,

each new one with a more desperate expression
in its face. And then more desperate again.
They have no gender, my sticks—

except sometimes I have pulled dugs out of a torso
and let them hang, while the stick sat cross-legged
like at a picnic, bent over its knees toward the earth.

12

When my mother was 80, she went into a nursing home.
I lied to her about where we were going,
though I never regretted telling that lie.
Sometimes I have trouble with how truth sounds.

Admission day is hard, not just for the admitted one.
Lots of lies are told that day. *If you don't like it,
you can come home.* That night, I made a vow. I was 45
and said, Not me. Not me—ever—in a nursing home.

My mother brushed away the hand of aides
who tried to feed her. My kind mother had forgotten
kindness, or even its appearance. She was mean
to everybody, even to her own children.
I found myself wishing for her death.

13

I think my boys want to put me in Ivy Hill.
Like mother like kid, I guess.
I'm not thinking too kindly
toward nursing homes, these days.
Remember how they called them "hotspots"
and all those old people were dying
during the pandemic?
I've told my boys there's no chance
they'll ever get me into a germ-infested
hotspot of a nursing home.

14

Mornings, I think about conversations
I've had with friends and strangers about
the "end of the trail."

Euphemisms are like allergic reactions
to the word death and like death, inevitable.
Euphemisms are a result of embarrassment.

My friends always agreed with me:
no way will *we* end up being fed at Ivy Hill,
or any nursing home, which they call "a warehouse."

Sometimes we'd think up methods. Ingestion
was always the first. I'd heard
of a woman who ate shoe polish.

And there're the ones who eat toadstools.
And of course there's hemlock, Socrates
and all that, though it's not the tree.

The hemlock that can do you in,
or *Conium maculatum,* is related
to the carrot. I knew Latin once.

Boyibus kissibus little girlorum.
Conium maculatum—just the sound of it is scary.
Patribus kickibus out through the doorum.

Sometimes hemlock's called "break-your-mother's-heart."

15

Give me a pill, doc, any day, a pill to end it.
It's easy to talk like that when you're healthy,
still have a driver's license,

you're continent and considering
the next new smart phone,
planning a garden for coming-on spring,

going to a grandchild's graduation,
meeting someone for dinner. Thing is,
a lot of my friends—the ones still around—

are *at* Ivy Hill, the very ones who said,
especially during COVID-19, that they'd
never end up in a nursing home.

A few of my friends have fallen in love again
and married or moved in with some needy type.
They've put off thinking about "end of life."

That conversation doesn't fit in
when you've rediscovered a certain friskiness
in yourself. Me, I swim. And I take Max for walks.

16

Do I still believe what we used to say?
My kids have had my license revoked.
I've asked them not to visit.

They'll see that I sometimes forget things
on the stovetop. Or leave the oven on all night.
Too bad. But my oven isn't Sylvia Plath's.

It wouldn't do me any good to stick
my head into an electric oven. Electricity.
Electricity. If it's not in use, turn off the juice.

But I forget sometimes. I know my boys are scheming
to get me into Ivy Hill. They tell me
I talk out loud to myself. I tell them I'm talking to Max.

I tell them the best way for me to work things out
when I'm contemplating is to talk to Max. Someone's
always listening, I say, but my boys don't want to hear.

And that's too bad. They used to listen.
I want to remember them the way I want them to be.
It helps to look out my windows.

I go over the question again and again:
Do I believe what we used to say?
Yes. Yes, I do. Never. Not me.

Sometimes, I start crying for no reason.
Strange, because tears don't come easily
when you get old. Some of my friends

haven't cried in years.
Decades.
Even at funerals.

17

Creepy-looking Dr. Kevorkian
should never have gone to jail.
He must have had terrible lawyers.

Dr. Death was a perfect name for him.
They called it "assisted suicide" back then.
Now they want it to be "assisted dying."

That might have helped Dr. Death.
But he had a point. A person
should be allowed to decide when it's over.

There are some states where you can do just that
and get a doc to give you the right amount.
Docs know those things.

But I wouldn't want a doc around me.
Not even a famous one like Dr. Death,
especially a famous one like Dr. Death.

Death is a time for solitude.

18

What Peter's father did remained with me,
from kindergarten on, an abstract now,
but not so much that I haven't begun

to think a rope might be the best option.
There's good rope and bad. Hemp. Sisal. Nylon.
But where do you attach it?

Surely a rod in a closet wouldn't hold.
And how do you make a noose anyway?
I know something of knots.

learned their intricacies as a child.
I wasn't a sailor. I just wanted to learn how to make knots.
So I asked for a book that would teach me.

I learned the beauty of tying, of uniting
one thing to another, and yet a noose
by the very sound of the word—those two o's—

frightens me, as if I were still a five-year-old learning
about Peter's father in the closet. And of course,
there's the chair—or should it be a stepladder?

Would I give it a balanced push, enough to send it
out of reach? The temptation may be to fail.
Peter's father had the touch I'd have to learn.

What *is* the physics here? The neck breaks.
But what if there's nothing so final as fracture?
The body might be taken down too soon

by someone who hears Max bark.

19

I've never pulled a trigger.
I remember mealtimes.
Through the kitchen window
my father would see
a *goddam* woodchuck
in the orchard.
Hannah, go get my gun.

Out the back door,
he'd blow shot
into that woodchuck,
return and pick up
where he'd left off at the table:
meatloaf, corn pudding,
beets from the garden.
How fortunate we are, he'd say,
how blessed, to have
such good food on the table,
while fur and guts lay in a red pile
beside an apple tree.

20

Where do you buy a gun anyway?
There used to be a gun shop on Route 5.
The guy who owned it was a rich kid,
an heir trying not to be a snob,
even when he shot skeet.

His shop is gone now like all the old places
on that highway. There are strip malls,
a Dari-Queen, a Subway, and that awful Ivy Hill.
The road is much wider now.

I'm clueless about ammunition.
How do you know what kind of bullets to buy?
What goes into those cylinders or the magazine well?
And what about a background check?
What would they find out about me?
That I dye my hair?
That I stole a spoon from Schrafft's?
That when I was 21, I lied my way

into the British Embassy to see Queen Elizabeth?
Could a person like that be trusted with a gun?

And the noise. I hear it in my head.
I see it: brains and hair against the wall,
like a dead woodchuck. Boom.

21

Flashback: When I was a newlywed,
I heard about an old man
who threw a radio into the tub
where his wife was bathing.
Plugged into an outlet on the bathroom wall.
The wire must have been just long enough.
I thought of the Rosenbergs
and the artfulness of electricity.
The man then put a gun
into his mouth and blasted himself
to the other side of the bathroom.
These two were tight. They had a pact.
A good marriage.
Tony and I didn't make pacts.

22

I drink vodka every day, not till afternoon,
of course, straight, no tonic, no vermouth,
no ice. And when I wake up at three o'clock or four

in the morning, I don't blame the five or six shots
I've had. It's my shoulder. It aches from swimming laps.
Or maybe from when Max tugs on his leash.

I can't sleep with pain. I worry about not sleeping,
but that makes me not sleep even more.
I walk around in the dark and end up where the pills are.

I take two or three. I take more than two or three.
I wash them down with vodka.
I wash the pills down with vodka.

Sleep would come with vodka,
and a plastic bag over the head.
Max on the floor beside my bed.

If it was winter and there was snow on the ground,
I'd take my clothes off, go outside
and lie down in the snow. Sleep would come

with vodka and snow.

23

Flashback: Tony died fast
like my grandmother.

He was out on his bike
for exercise, rode every day,

usually just after dawn.
I was getting breakfast

when he came in one morning
and said, *air's heavy today.*

Under the showerhead
he slid slowly down

into the tub while water pelted
his essence into the drain.

Tony isn't in heaven.

Flashback: I knew

about the woman in the pink
angora sweater. Sweetness

and warmth, no interests
other than to see to Tony's ease.

I was 60 then, on a roll with my sticks.
I've always wanted to make a stick

that was suffering from heavy air.
Head bowed, shoulders low.

Resolve on the face, a calm
signifying there is no afterlife,

no heaven, Tony.

24

I love this song.
        È giunta mezzanotte,
        si spengono i rumori,
        si spegne anche l'insegna
        di quell'ultimo caffè.
A Parisian in tails late at night walks
along the Seine. It could've been Rome,
but it wasn't. The words are Italian.
But the scene is Paris.

And by the last verse
the man's hat is floating on the river.
So is the gardenia that was in his lapel.
He's gone. That's why I sing only
the first verse. Till now, that is.
I've thought it was better to stay
with a first verse of tragedy
than to get to the end.
But now I wonder: was it really tragic?
Maybe he was just an old Parisian,
an old person like me. He dressed
for the occasion,
knew what he was going to do.

25

There's a bridge not too far from here.
It's a big old steel construction
with struts and trusses, rivets and girders.
I don't know if I'd be able
to climb the railing. Boats
go back and forth beneath it,
not big ones. But it's a busy river.
Tony had a friend whose father
had made some terrible error at work,
cost the company millions,
and so he jumped from a bridge
into a New York City river.
Don't know which one. But it
seems he couldn't do anything right.
He landed on a sailor in a scow
and killed the poor guy.
How can we ever be certain
of not hurting another person?

26

Recently in the outdoor city pool
I tried to suck water into my body
through my nose and into my lungs.

I didn't put rocks down my bathing suit
or do anything Virginia Woolf-like.
No real drama. Just practice, though

there was something familiar about it.
Water to water—
beginning and end, full circle.

A palindrome, like my name. Hannah.
Hannah Hyatt O'Reilly.
H-two-O

Well, a sniff is all it took, and I felt
the liquid enter my nose, causing me to almost smell
something under my brow. Or was it pain?

I coughed chlorine. My sounds shot up,
staccato, pizzicato, with splash and panic.
My arms flailed, and I swam over poolside

where a skimmer bobbed sucking up the litter
of a city's summer. A lifeguard from her tall chair
looked down at me and called out.

I couldn't hear what she said,
though by then I'd stopped sputtering,
having learned what desperation

mixed with instinct under water
would make me do: thrust myself up
from the deep, the way a newborn

pushes out from its mother, in an urgency
of abandoning water for oxygen.
I'm not trying to be born

27

I'm not trying to be re-born either.
But let's say I actually die.
I signed a paper years ago, signed myself
right into the word *cremation*.

See how the *m* has inserted itself
into *creation*? Take it out
and I could start all over again.

But would I? I was a third girl, they wanted
a boy. I came during the World Series,
and they left me in the hospital nursery
while they listened to the game on the radio.

No, if I were to create myself again—
I'd start out later than that, older.
Like I wouldn't mind a romp in bed

with someone good at it like Tony.
Someone who'd bring me gardenias
and tell me I smelled of Tahiti.

I wouldn't mind holding a newborn again
(without the fatigue, mastitis, the weight gain).
I wouldn't mind finding my art earlier.

But I'd skip the middle time,
when the kids have their own cars
and seldom utter any words,

and then all of a sudden, they're living
with someone, doing their own creating,
going to baby showers,
parent-teacher conferences and graduations,

all the while the *m* is encroaching fast
like a comet arcing. It inserts itself into *creation*
effortlessly, laying the kindling, wadding up the news,
and striking the match.

28

Starvation could be the answer.
At my age, it can't take long.

But I love to eat. Tony loved to eat, too.
We had a lot in common like that,

more than coincidence,
although I love coincidence—

like the time I was reading a poem
in a magazine and found myself in it,

right there in the poem.
About a woman named Hannah,

who walks her dog, a black lab named Max,
and puts a newspaper under him when the time comes.

She's quick, discreet, "graceful in her swoop,"
is how the poet put it, "conscious of creature privacy"

and wanting to protect nature in a city of cars
and klaxons—that's the poet's word.

Turns out the poet lives nearby,
sees me at the pool and on my walks with Max.

Soon he's going to notice how emaciated I'm getting,
how slow my pace. He's going to stop me.

How are you, Hannah?
and he'll hand me a bag of Fritos.

Later, but not much, Max and I will no longer go for walks.
Poets ask a lot of questions. But they don't get many answers.

They guess at a lot of things. They make things up.
But they don't lie. Our poet will notice Hannah's absence,

and he'll remember how thin she was last time he saw her.
And where's the dog for goodness' sake?

That slow and serious old dog, Max.
He'll ask that question over and over. But of himself,

deep in the inner workings of his poet-heart,
he'll ask where the old woman could possibly be.

He'll never get the answer,
and eventually he will ring our bell.

He's holding a casserole. He's standing straight
at the door downstairs, he's waiting to be buzzed in.

2 Split

I am not I.
    I am this one
walking beside me whom I do not see . . .

    Juan Ramón Jiménez
    Translated by Robert Bly

Daisy Chain

Diagnosis: schizophrenia

Ellie, Ellie, saffron Ellie
picks daisies easy
eats pizza at Pistelli's
Ellie laughs
broad girl-lips
carries the daisy chain with friends

Ellie, Ellie, woman Ellie
sallower now begins to split
Ellie here Ellie there
half an Ellie grabs an Ellie
keeps her inside
ever fewer months a year

finds an Ellie
in a pocket
dot staccato
in a pocket
she'd forgotten
and another in a locket

tattered words of katydids
thrown from deep-brown Ellie-throat
pickatale tinkerpail
till there's no going back
Ellie   Ellie   Ellie/Ellie

And Everything Nice

Spices in my kitchen cabinet
have to be in alphabetical order.
Think OCD, if you must.

The C's—most hard, some soft—
win hands down.
Cardamom, cayenne, caraway,

curry, cloves, cumin, coriander,
celery salt, cinnamon,
chilies and chives.

The dill stands alone. The dill stands alone.
Heigh-ho the derry O,
rosemary, too.

And nutmeg. Beware the nutmeg.
It has psychoactive myristicin
that'll launch you beyond Thanksgiving.

Taste it with me, my pretty.
And show me how to get into the oven.

On Seeing *Psycho* in a Concert Hall

The orchestra begins to play.
The screen out of certain bravery
hangs high in the hall.

We all know what's going to happen,
because memory is swirling
in this place tonight, reaching back

to when it felt good to tremble,
back to drive-ins, re-runs,
rainy nights, and sleepovers.

And the music, the strings—
you know they're going to climb
higher and higher, until they squeak,

screech, cricket-shrill into your body,
and you hear and see, absorbed
into your past, into the bygone night

of a film that's risen again
from a dead man's mind,
into a steamy shower, into murder,

and blood, and water in the drain.
When it stops, it does not stop.
Even the musicians crane their necks,

believing in the sounds they've made,
turning their eyes up to the screen, to take in,
like us, what they've been accomplices to.

Ciao to Solonghello

A town in Piemonte, Italy, pop. 212

Welcome to ambivalence,
place of being and unbeing,
hello-goodbye,
push-me-pull-you's of the mind's crossroads.
I look in one direction
toward reluctance and nostalgia
and in the other
toward invention and risk.
I am the moon. I am the sun.
I am the past. I am to be.
So it goes.
Ciao, I say. *I'm leaving now.*
Ciao, I say. *I'm back again.*
Leavingnowbackagain.
Backagainleavingnow.
So long, hello, Solonghello.

What They Say About Suicide

They say he did it out of his own choosing,
just over the line there, down
into the Piedmont, they say, down

into the lake where he drowned.
They say he did it to join his wife
and children, who'd died in a fire.

Better spit on the ground three times for luck.
Death robs you of your own creations,
they say, say it pushes the speed of wind

to new limits, fusses with the pull of currents,
adjusts heat over frigid waters. Death causes.
Death swallows, chews, they say.

Death decides when you can do something
out of your own choosing.

The Sig Poems

in memory of Sigmund S.

Sig's Cars

Police cars sentenced me to damnation in Colorado.
Police gun cars threw me into the hospital.

Two cops tore my arms out across the front of a police car
and broke both my shoulders, downstream and no shoes.

Corporations work through police cars.
Time magazine hunts cars.

Time advertises what they will hunt.
Many days they followed my car.

I was five cars stolen. I have no car.
I walk to serious leg and eye consequences.

They hunted me all around Oakland, California.
Department radios posted everywhere.

That's him!

From the speed of cars and telephones,
I know there's something beyond us.

Sig Talks Himself into a Brawl and the Police Come

Listen listen, Sig, listen,
glisten to me, Tristan,
to the voices voices choices
in Arkansas I saw
now do it do it do hit the guy
who's looking at you.
Hit 'im, Sig. Hit 'im, Sig.
Take me, Siren, beauty dame,
your song is playing in my head,
Siren lures me cures me blurs me.
I forget my esses. Inanity.
Sigmund. Who named me Sigmund?
I forget my esses. I am Igmund.
I get one phone call. That's all.

Sig's Injuries

The story of my beatings
by police is thin and bandaged.
I was no names.

I was no names. At school,
we were good times.
Touch football, squadron good sport.

I was no names.
Now my head is kicked in.
I won't ski again,

terrible end
to a literary beginning
at school. I went home

to Mother. In a house.
In a room. In a shelter.
With contusions, injuries,

thin and bandaged,
head kicked in. Good sport.
I was no names.

Sig's Letter to His Old Friend the Lawyer

Good days to you and legal world.
Boarded Greyhound in Houston.
Not a good letter.
In two days I was in the trees
on a side road in Arkansas,
police revolver behind my head,
me, in the trees. Scarce legal help.
Not a good letter. Can't write it all down,
and too much of it is screamed.
My back is ruined, neck broken.
Brain, shot full of bone & cartilage.
Black Shirts drove me to the morgue.
Not dead. Not a good letter.
All the best to you in Legal City.

A Mental Health Hospital Closes

Where have they been left?
On the streets—in shelters—
in jails—on trains.

Sidewalk grate, warm thyself.

The 1,810 windows are shut tight.
The doctor once said views from windows
were made for healing. Lovely leas cure.

Landscape, paint thyself.

It's dangerous to cross the tracks. Signals
are malfunctioning near Hubbell and Claypool.
They're riding the trains. They've got the bindle.

Will work for food,
will sleep for good. Who?
The eastbound ramp to Hubbell is closed,

as if by a rock at the mouth of a cave
where bats hang all day and at night fly
into the closed-down building.

The 1,030 doors led to heart chambers
that heaved with anguish in the 550 rooms.
A lone bat hangs in the corner of the 3rd-floor hallway.

Building empty. Where have they gone?
A burglar has died of asphyxiation in a jail cell.
A murderer of six relatives is on trial.

A voice told him to kill them.
So the people will kill him
by lethal injection on a gurney.

Hospital, heal thyself.

Firefighters were called to a small flare on the grass
behind Home Depot. Beware small flares.
Firefighters can't get there fast enough.

The eastbound ramp to Hubbell is closed.

Homeless

Remember the old draft? 1A,1Y, 4F?
There will always be a Vietnam.
You're looking for your leg. All around,
the seen and the missing—like the child
outside the movie house, kidnapped.
The asylum on the hill will not let you in.
All refuge is closed and taking water into its lungs.
They're buying insurance on the exchange
or pot in Denver. Meth among the tweakers.
You have some place to sleep tonight.
You do, don't you? Always a Canada, too.
Fighting—good for business.
Fighting—good business.
Every day you fall out of the WTC
into the construction site below, the abyss,
where religions fight in the name of religion
reflected in a pool. God kills. You know that,
but all human beings are not created equal.
The boy pulls a trigger again and again
in Newtown and Kabul, no difference in guns.
You sleep on a grate, covered in eaten blankets
looking for your leg, listening for a siren.

Good-Luck Bin

Each day it yielded
something she would need.
This time a diamond earring
sparkled on the walk
just beside the bin. She squinted
at its brilliance,
bent to pick it up,
stem askew, golden setting dented.
It'd be safe in her pocket, safe
from heavy feet
of those with scraps
and clods to toss.
She never wondered
if the diamond trod upon was real,
never wondered
how it happened to be biding there
amid the grit beside the bin,
where she came daily shod
in worn-out running shoes,
not knowing whose they'd been,
nor was she curious.

By Reason of Insanity

"World's too much with us, too effin' much
with us." She spoke inside her head, as she sauntered

out the gate at St. Elizabeth's, looking visitor-like
to the guard, who nodded with that have-a-good-one kind of look.

Third time in recent weeks a guard had let a patient-prisoner walk out
into freedom, which goes by the name of city traffic,

pollution, intersection, elevator, subway, bench, and burger,
probably a Bud, a Dos Equis with a lime, a wine cooler.

"Late and soon" confused her, chronologically, rhymes with
hate the moon, ate the balloon, last thing she'd bought for him—

purple, buoyant, shiny—before she bound him with duct tape
and held him under in the tub and counted to six

for the number of years he'd lived. And another six
for one to grow on. And another six, bringing him into his teen years

when of course he'd turn into something crazy, like a killer
with guns and semi-automatic rifles, blazing into a kindergarten.

Damn, I'm laying waste my powers, I mean, I'm looking for God,
I mean, I'm looking for a taxi.

Needles

I drop him off at acupuncture
for the hair-thin needles
that will alleviate the pain
in his knee. Blocks
down from there, outside
the psychiatric clinic,
I'm waiting at a red light
contemplating what walking is,
how down is harder
on the knees than up,

when I see an ambulance
at the clinic door
and two men pushing
a gurney at the curb
with a woman prone,
strapped, inert. I drive away,
as if I'd dropped *her* off too,
left her to lie in a room,
where someone will administer

a thick syringe filled
with what will hide her pain,
keep it at bay, while
a bluish breeze eddies
through an open window,
sucks a playful curtain
out into the closed-off world,

.

Waiting for a Train: A Man with a Plan

A palindrome goes both ways.

Snub no man, I heard him say.
He turned to look at me
at the dead-end platform bay.

Nice cinnamon buns, I heard him say.
Was he coming on to me as prey?
He held out pastries.

I looked the other way.
Snub no man, again I heard him say.
Nice cinnamon buns.

He stared at me and offered me
an array of yeasty sweets.
Would next it be café au lait?

I snubbed him and his tray of eats.
Again he cautioned, *snub no man*,
and he sashayed in front of me,

from right to left and left to right and
to and fro, with his buffet,
backward, forward. He didn't stray—

no, his beginning was the end,
the end, his start again.
Snub no man. Nice cinnamon buns,

he said once more, threw out a laugh,
as into, out of himself he passed,
north and south, forth and back,

like the train screeching in the bay
coming toward us, then back away,
in its own course of road ballet.

Emma's Appointment with a Psychiatrist

A split has broken through,
and all the minikins
in her brain are rioting
out and back in and out again.

It's as if a ruff annoys
her chin, as if a sheaf of hay
scratches her eyes. Earwigs
scurry-squirm under her waist.

Seated in a chair next to her,
the doctor keeps on asking.
But there's only silence
in a dry-as-dust office.

A sourdine has muted her
or changed her tone. Alone
she pulls between strings
at a sound of peace in the gut.

Swing Time

Even after dusk had drained into darkness
and a chill had lowered itself onto them
covering the playground—slide,
seesaw in perfect balance,
jungle gym, his hair and hers—
she wasn't tired of pushing him
in that lightless place
where swing chains whined.
She pushed him, pushed him,
continued to push   push   push
and stopped every so often to ensure
that he was napping safe within his arc.

Pigeon

for an old friend

With deadening meds,
you didn't imitate his gait,
as you would have once
to make us laugh. Full of meds
you didn't scratch the sidewalk
or hunch your shoulders,
crest your elbows, blink, bob, or coo.
Instead, you stumbled
toward a bench, sat down
almost motionless, until your hand
slowly proffered corn toward his beak.
Did you share his cravings?
Recognize them from the way
he cocked his face
sideways up toward you?
and took the grain as if accepting
payment for a flight
over what was reachable to you
in other days. We stayed,
just you and I, for a few moments
in the expanse of it. But you?
You rose and followed
the pigeon aloft, curling
those beautiful legs of yours
under your belly
and in slow motion.
I had to let you go.

Stuart Among the Nightingales

based on a newspaper story out of Ohio

After the pruners dropped out of the maples
and beeches, packed up their ropes, saws,
and harnesses into the truck laden with trimmings
and logs, they drove away.

The woman in the house waved goodbye
from an upstairs window, smiling
in the absence of buzz-saw. But Stu, star climber,
came back. He knew she'd left the side door open.

He entered, was putting her gold watch
into his pocket when she appeared
in the kitchen. He smiled at her. He raped her.
He killed her with his bowie.

What next? He knew how to climb, and more,
how to slice, saw, chop, disentangle, split, sever and pull.
He'd been intimate with this woman's trees,
particularly the beech going rotten and hollow.

So he carried the cut-up body outside in a bag
and up into the dying tree, where the birds
now stilled their dusk sounds. He lowered the bag
into the wound of the trunk, where heartwood

and cambium were turning to dust, insects
masticating, running lengths among the pulp
that teemed in slow decay. He stayed there,
perched high inside the copper canopy, where leaves

quivered their lament for the limbs they'd lost that day.

The Heel Stone at Stonehenge

One theory: the shadow of the Heel Stone at sunrise
symbolizes fertilization "of the Earth Mother by the Sky Father
at the height of his power on the longest day."

To be an outlier is to be the Heel Stone,
unable to enter the circle, aging,
eroding, corroding, and gradually,
imperceptibly, leaning
in all weathers and seasons
on that breathtaking plain.
Listing like that, it's as if melancholy
has taken him by the shoulders.
But he's not sad to be on the outside,
at least most of the time. He knows
that the upright stones in the circle
will never make room for him,
try as he might to enter.
Isolation makes him contemplative.
Makes him aware. Makes him
stand tall unabashedly for inclusion
and love. Makes him look around
at all the good things
on the plain. Makes him eager
for the sunrise of the longest day,
when his shadow will penetrate the circle,
even if he can't.

Collection de l'Art Brut

Lausanne, Switzerland

The creator
cannot stop,
has to express
beyond all limits.
The horse
of bark and branches,
born out of necessity,
tears through wind,
and the wind rips
through the horse
in this place
of the innermost.
What escapes
from within the unwalled
is imprisoned
inside the paddock.

Horse Dress, 1939

She wore the horse she'd crocheted
out of scraps of bright wool.
No pattern. Needlework
so exquisite the horse's eyes fit
perfectly at her nipples, as if
she were looking for someone
to cup her and comfort her
during her paces around corridors,
in circles, bound by fences, walls,
lanes to stay in, tail trailing
like an extension of her coccyx.

Snout and nostrils covered her groin.
She must've craved a carrot
or an apple, Eve's,
that would free her, make her able to love,
be loved, to misjudge, to err,
to misspeak, to know things, to unite
opposites running naked inside her.

Nurses tried to stop her from wearing the horse.
One of her voices said, no, the very one
that had bullied her
into taking up the crochet hook.

Disposing of a Dress, 1957

At the stern, she began to take off
the dark blue-and-white cotton dress.

A *becoming* dress, her mother had often said
in the way mothers had

of braiding praise around censure
and control under love, weaving and unweaving,

praise and censure and control and love
around her head and body

as she untangled the swaddling
on shipboard and cast it out into an ocean.

I Am Not Joan Rivers

But will someone, please, impersonate me?
I want to look at myself in the flesh—

see my right hand as a right hand,
my left as a left. Impossible in mirrors.

Reflection cannot contain periphery.
When my eye looks to one side,

I want to see real edges and shores,
to gather what's there, watching you be me.

You must be slightly younger,
so you'll stay longer and remind of laughter.

I want you to have light brown hair
and good thighs, smooth arms, thick eyebrows.

I want you to whistle at times,
usually while you stand at the sink.

I want you to sing songs that get stuck
in your head for hours and hours.

I want you to play the bugle. Taps at sundown.
Taps at Arlington. Taps for your father and mother.

You'll do things I won't recognize,
things you've seen me do I don't know I'm doing.

you may even hurt someone with words.
You will know who and why. I won't.

Insecure in an Age of Synthesis

a convolute

Hiding behind kiosks,
I'm magnifying my voice.
I am not synthetic.

I'm patient, using my words,
trying to acclimate to the culture.
I have made sunsets pinker, oceans bluer.

Sometimes it's the simplest changes
that make the biggest impact.
I can't decide between up and down.

I'm trying to light the room on fire,
let life in, ignite the light, catch the light.
One of my biggest fears right now is not finding it.

I am not synthetic. I'm looking
for something at the deli, a less savage place.
I have to be firm in my search.

I walk in, sit, smile slowly.
I should try the grocery store.
This is about taste. And that can be catastrophic

like the reaction of young women to Zika.
Or voters who want authenticity.
I love their sense of irreverence.

They deflect with humor things that just don't feel right.
especially in the gray days of winter.
It makes no sense to talk about climate change.

Echo of the Frogs

It was never quiet in my mind,
always a rill mowing the shale I shattered
for trilobites—anything to remember time.

A bug, let's say, in a glob of resin.
Amber. Color makes the name.
Amethyst. But my name is not Amethyst

after the brooch of purple circled with pearls.
It looked the way she smelled—
like her dresser drawer sachet.

Silken, my mother smelled of chanterelle and Chanel.
I have no name to sell or put a price on. Withaney.
I'll call myself Withaney—that's what's left of me.

Memory is fossil now, piece of mirror-quartz.
Look into the surface of a pond, not a pond *invented*
like the lakes we see on what was once a farmer's lea,

built up with columns and Palladian windows looking out
on driveways circling counterfeit redoubts.
The *honest* pond, fed by streams, by snows and rains,

always filled in spite of drought, assassinations,
coups d'état, and marriages. Some things *do* last entirely.
I look deep inside the honest pond and see myself,

Withaney, in silt among the frogs. She's dead
and she is rotted leaves. The stream of youth flows
through web-veins, oozes with them into bog.

Her frailty, too, slowly creeps like glacial ice
slippery over gneiss, geology of time. What went through
her mind when she lit up a cigarette at 14?

She had no clue that frogs awaited her
or that she'd find herself in earth as well
as in the air and on the sea. Gardenias. Remember

how they turned brown on teenage wrists?
but still their scent was sweet
on into morning's light? Even of a moon.

*

Fire and combustion are other stories. Men and women
built legacies, and scion names were smelted
into a hundred billion coins, now ashy residue.

They die and died of drink and gout, crashed in Bugattis
and Piper Cubs, fell from mansion balconies, lay bitten in the jungle
where they went for art. Withaney doesn't cry at expensive tragedy.

They die and live like the pond's reflection—on the surface.
They avoid frogs' mud, won't swallow algae
or get their hair wet. Death comes to all depths.

Most will never see the frogs. Assassination is an answer.
Or war. Kill is the imperative. Muster. Then play Taps.
Sacrifice is highly overrated.

The frog is Atlas, holding up the pond's reflection,
which is the universe. Call him Maha Manduka, but
be grateful to the mirror for revealing to us our appearance only.

*

At the summer equinox, the curious quail sees herself as a frog,
ever so briefly, but she learns and keeps within her what it's like
beneath the surface of the dark water.

She returns to her covey for the night, and the birds sleep circularly
like herdsmen around the fire, their heads facing out into the dark.
Beneath water, the frog swims until he climbs into the grasses

beside the rill to pant good fortune or to catch an insect.
But when he starts to croak his words, his puns, his jokes,
he's not Earth's sound, but Withaney's brother,

the infant she cradled when she was ten, the infant
she swaddled, the waddler, the screamer, the delight,
eventually the seated figure looking out a window.

There are stories on the bottom of the honest pond.
They are rotting leaves, dead twigs, and acrid mud.
They are the pollywogs of me, the frogs of me.

This morning a full moon turned a sunset orange
as I watched it fall behind the trees into the southern sky.
July two-o will come again and again for many lives.

Only a few more times for me. Still, I have the memory
of youth in 1969, when I watched a moon undergo
the unexpected blow of visitors from outer space.

Water on the Moon

a convolute

Walmart parking lot, at least eight bodies
in a tractor-trailer. At least 38 people
in the back of the trailer, believed
to be suffering heatstroke or dehydration,
asking for water, trace amounts of water,
deep within the moon's "wet" interior,
asking for water deep within the trailer truck.

At least twenty in critical condition,
seven hospitals. Others of less severity
believed to be asking for water, ice,
in shadowed regions at the lunar poles,
"water that you can get on the moon
instead of bringing with you."
At least eight bodies including two children.

Heart rates over 130 beats per minute,
very hot to touch, energy emitted by
the moon's hot surface. **Asking for water.**
Bodies including two children. No signs
of water inside, no signs
of trapped water, ice. Footage of vehicles
arriving to pick up some survivors.

Others on foot may have managed
to escape into the woods nearby, believed
to be asking for water **in a shadowed region.**

Cold Space

His body—wrinkle-dark
after a week or two on the floor
of a lifeless living room—

stayed for thirty days more
in a morgue refrigerator
until the sister was located,

identified it, okayed cremation,
and buried the ashes
next to the graves of their parents,

who would never learn their first-born
had become a misanthrope.
But *we* knew it.

We neighborhood kids
knew it way back in those early days.
He was the kind of big brother

you stayed away from, the kind that
eavesdropped on teenage conversations
and let us know we were nothing more

than disposable, like what's forgotten
for a month or two in the crisper drawer—
limp leaf of lettuce, slimy green bean.

Louisa Reads the Inside Cover
of a Poetry Magazine
for Louisa Newlin

When she saw Stephen Sandy's name
on that inside cover, where they put a death or two
every month, she remembered the day
he came from Robert Lowell's class
into the fiction class she was taking.

Lowell had left unexpectedly for the whole semester.
Lowell did a lot of things unexpectedly in those days.
Stephen and all of Lowell's other poet-students
poured into the fiction class, and the memory
made her laugh. A poet can't do fiction—

anybody knows that. Even when poets lie,
they're telling the truth, which may not be the truth
at the time. Someday, maybe. Eventually the truth
belongs to the living. As for the dead, Stephen,
she and you prepared well in fiction.

So, how can we be sure you are truly dead?

3 Threatened

What syllable are you seeking,
Vocalissimus,
In the distances of sleep?
Speak it.

from Wallace Stevens, *Harmonium*

Threat

You know better than anyone
how it games your mind
takes your brain in its hands
pulses at it sculpts it kneads it
into abstraction displays it
sometimes spotlights it
advertises it in a catalog of shapes
rides it with the top down
gives it for a price
or gives it to an unchosen
who becomes chosen, or else.

Sign: Fragile Roof

At times your feet feel securely planted
on the stairs—not so much, perhaps, on your way

from the basement, but beginning with the first floor
where food is stirred, puréed, and brought to a boil.

There your feet handle well the risers. Hungry,
you arrive at the floor where you sit at table.

And then you go on up to where living's done
on sofas and where fires heat and light the walls.

And ever moving up, with confidence you reach
the floor for sleeping and making love,

unless you were so moved before on earlier floors,
since both can be had in any room of any house.

Up and up—and now you limp—until you reach
whole lath and shingles fallen in among

the unused chairs and broken hobby horses.
Tax returns and diaries in boxes,

trunks, valises, and there the summer clothes
as if the season will return.

Through decay and openings in the fragile roof
you look into the leaf-less trees outside

and into clouds gray and full of snow, doubtful
you should venture onto any roof that has opened

its maw to lure you, suck you back
into something less than paradise.

Mimosa

Easter for her was a crash
into the carpet store window.
She'd been full of the idea
of resurrection that she'd seen
in the grape hyacinths
as she drove down Springfield Avenue
after brunch with the boys.
She loved going to their house.
They were both needlepointing
with the finest threads
postage-stamp size art pieces
that she looked at
through a magnifying glass.
She delighted in microcosm.
And the mimosas were good, too,
the color of crocuses
in front of Siegel's Stationery.
Easter had filled her with such joy
she took her eye off the road,
and the carpet store window
was now broken over her car
in minute pieces, each reflecting
a facet of her face
behind the windshield,
blood on her blouse.
Siren, she thought,
or am I thinking Risen?

Miniature Book Collection

The books stack up, high,
miniature high, in inches
of miniature stories.

All stories end up miniature,
though it's easy to forget
how small they are

like children who never
got to hear their own
miniature stories.

Stories add up
like gunshot deaths,
one here, one there.

No one takes notice
until the massacre,
and miniature horror is made large

until it is miniature again.

The Miniaturist, 1828

Sarah Goodridge (1788-1853)

When she heard his wife had died,
she painted a miniature self-breast,
with which he was surely familiar—

he whose name Daniel Webster had burst out
huge into the public consciousness.
He did not ask her to join him in the forum.

She was a mere painter of large things
made small, not so much insignificant,
as causing the naked eye to squint.

She continued to live off the minuscule,
the pocketable, in her unimportant way,
but no customer gave her workspace the shiver
he had brought about among her paints.

Life without ecstasy left her woeful.
He remarried. Someone else. She was certain
he would destroy the miniature, the two baby birds,

craning, eager in their nest. But history revealed
he'd locked it in a drawer, as if
the quick click of a key could keep a secret.

Quiet Air

Come back, wind, the old man cries,
hearing everything he's not heard
since the last windless day when he lurched
naked into the pine forest in search
of the missing Boreas he loved,
protective tumult that curled
inside his walls, into his pockets, his ears.

In wind's absence now he hears
the drips of faucets, insects' s-sounds
against the sides of glass.
The pendulum drums out tock in the front hall
like a gong around a giraffe's neck.

He begs Elsa to tie him into a wicker rocker
on the porch where he'll wait out the lull.
Come back, wind, he cries out again

and again, rocking in frenzy.

Winter Night, a Lullaby

I will wreak silence on engines of the night,
deny air to fighter jets and propellers,
all road to sirens, radios, and worn brake pads.

I will guard the snowy street from plows
that in sparks rasp the frozen pitch-asphalt
intruding into your sleep as they assault

winter's soundless intention to turn surfaces
into tender white contours, to hide sly angles
of distraction, sharp geometries.

I will rock you, flush-warm child,
who's been woken by invention,
so that you will hear the song.

Empty Beds

Beds are crying themselves
to sleep in this forgotten era,

if sleep comes at all
to beds that can't afford a doctor

or the price of learning,
or a gun-less room,

to beds that have lost their job
or their pension, or beds

unable to trust neighbors
behind the scrim,

or beds that fear dying for a lie
or being exiled for the truth.

Beds meet dawn in chaos,
sheeted-sweaty, sheeted-curled,

and at an angle to the wall.
Desperate beds cannot

open doors, cannot walk out
into a reddish dawn.

Fire!

Remembering the Clinton, NY, arena, which burned on September 11, 1953

It's a date this village does not forget,
just hours after a fight.

One of the boxers had no place to go,
so he settled down for a night
in the arena stands on a pile of clothes.

He was asleep, when smoke
made him bolt up from a dream of handshakes,
haymakers, broken noses, contusions.

He yelled *Fire!*
to all the fans who were not there.
Fire! Fire! Fire! Run for your lives.

And he ran. He ran for the door, yelling,
listening to his own voice in the vacant arena,
just to know he was still standing for the count.

Yet, *Fire!* in an empty place
contains no sound within itself.

Fire in the Pale Green Bedroom

for Lilliane

1 *Before the Fire*

I've seen you at 93 or -4, in your pale green bedroom,
sitting by the window, the view west sailing smoothly
over trees and rooftops, especially in wintertime
when you watch the fire-red sunset and think about
your brother at 17 in January of 1941.

Torpedoed on the high seas.

And you at 16, already safe from the Nazis,
your parents, too. But your brother's ship never arrived.

2 *During the Fire*

A din at dawn, an alarm pierces the air. I put my winter coat on
over my nightgown, go into the hallway. I hear your voice.

Your door is open. There you are in your foyer. Your bathrobe blue.
You're on the phone with 911. Your bedroom's on fire. I run to look.

The pale green room is flames halfway to the ceiling, silent flames,
orange/white flames, butterfly flames starting their migration,

gathering speed, gathering color, heat, a spread of wings.
Take your walker, quick, hurry. We must get out.

3 *The Day after the Fire*

Your pale green bedroom is gone now, your home is soot and water.
You cannot go back. You are displaced, without clothes or photos,
without identification, without a name on a piece of paper,

nothing to prove who you are—a woman of 94 years, who loves art,
reads newspapers, has had an array of orchids, a driver's license,
a passport that has always given her the freedom to stay or to leave.

Sleeplessness

Soundless comes at night,
streaming on cobwebs
from rafters
or across floorboards
and under the bed.
It never learned
a language, though
it quivers.
It never learned
to moan in a throat,
never learned to stomp
on stairs or pound a fist
against glass.
It can look through
its own transparency,
mere mime. It signs
with fingers that remain
unheard. Fiery mica
hides in surrounding rock,
the early side of day.

                    *

Middle night, the walls do not move.
The stairs rise silent and fall.
Not a paw twitches.

Not a light switch clicks.
The fish settle to lower inches
beside the castle.

Still, *I hear the humming of my blood.*

It throbs, ebbs, swarms through my arms
to my shoulders to my toes, into and out of
the heart of me,

pulsing hydrozoa, animal, insect, clock set
for six-thirty, tarsal-claws sturdy-splayed
supporting the dresser.

*

A spider, intruder of the secret kind,
as we lay separate in our bed two nights ago,

bit my arm. By morning at my wrist
a mound grew hot, angry-deep and red.

A flame will always die
but leave a shadow of itself.

Later in our morning sun, I smoothed the bed.
A blur of black swept across a pillowcase.

Between a tissue ready in my hand
I tracked it to its crunching end.

And yet last night as we lay side by side,
I knew it wasn't gone. There was a skittering

beneath the sheet, a tingling on my toes
up and over both my thighs—a presence

I knew I had to keep from you and me.
And when the swelling on my arm began to itch,

I also knew the presence had a name,
and so I scratched and scratched some more

in rhythm's rub, as if a song would keep us safe
from what was with us there.

Mutilation and Thanatosis

After sex
the male spider, *L. jeskovi,*
twists the female's scapus off
with his pedipalps.
There's nothing left
to hold on to.
Now no one
will get her.
Progeny secure
in a one-time coming,
mortal, like the sire's breath,
and the tears of the dam.

During sex
the male spider, *P. mirabilis,*
is known to fake his own death
so his mate won't kill him.
He lures her with a "nuptial gift,"
but holds on to it
even in death,
just in case
she has a mind
to run off with it
before his resurrection
when he can finish his job.

The crescent moon
sinks, and a star with it,
lowered into
hidden reverse forces.

Walt's Notebook

Bed 15

Bandages swaddle him.
Blanket stains curdle.
Wails lift to the crowded-room ceiling,
spread to the hospital walls
that enclose fever.

An orange, please.

I will get him an orange.
Tomorrow. I will squeeze it
into a cup, will hold the zest
to the boy's nose, let him smell
the leaves, bark, the pulp of it,
sun of the south. I will cup
the boy's nape into my hand
and hold a tin vessel to his lips.

Bed 59

Delirious, he wants liquorice.
Liquorice or horehound
or rock candy.
I'll bring him something
for his parched mouth,
something for him fevered
to suck that will
increase his saliva
into the sweetness of infant,
motherless, unable to walk,

guttural in his cries
for the comfort
of liquorice.

Whitman's Last Words

March 26, 1892

Warry, shift.
From bed,
he was asking something
of Warren, his nurse,
asking his nurse
to turn him over.
Maybe he said,
Adjust me, Warry.
Change things for me.
I'm not comfortable.
Not yet. Not now.
And then he said,
Warry, shift.
It's no good this way.
Warry, shift. Shift, Warry.
My weight. I feel it.
It wants to move,
alter its lie.
I feel my weight.
I don't feel my weight.
Get me ready, Warry.
Shift, Warry.

Joel & Tragedy: an Aubade

When we woke up today and you related
your dream about the lovers—

Lovely Tragedy Wilcox, Northumbrian detective,
and Frenchman, crack inspector, Joel Baudelaire—

I was aware something had happened
during our night together. Did a gun go off?

Did a car chase end in raucous clamor? Did Tragedy
slide in next to you, as I lay sleeping, my back

against your legs? Did Joel brush a finger across
my shoulder? And did you let him? Well, tell me,

did the two solve the felony? resolve the transgressions?
They sang "O Magnum Mysterium"—in falsetto, you said.

And as you left for work, there was quartz in your voice,
laughter in your spleen, spiral in your gait.

Ella at the Turn of the Century, 1900

Agnes is the cellist, Bess the violinist, Kate the pianist
> the teenage trio forged
> out of their mother Ella's mania.

She abandons them at times,
> to keeping house alone
> to practicing alone
> to putting up their posters in upstate farm villages.

The Bundy Sisters play granges and auditoriums
> while the century hollows out.
> Aughty-aught, the people say, terror
> on their tongues, and Ella quivers in a rest home.

The fear of a new era tastes yellow.

The girls draw close
> angle their heads like sparrows
> to listen, one to the others.

Over their cadences they can almost hear
> their mother's songs, her trills,
> her womanly treble
> as she flees naked into a neighbor's field
> with visions of ascent into Heaven
> on the right hand of God in 1901.

Urban Mourning

It didn't take long for the Easter chicks
to show signs of being roosters,
and I was no longer allowed to keep them.

My mother made me put them in a box
and drove me to Frank's Texaco station.
Frank's father had a chicken farm.

The station was across the street
from a funeral home, cypress-vertical,
beige-brick building on a corner, where

it awaited the expected and unexpected
needs for its mysterious inner services—
like my grandmother's funeral.

I took the chick box into the station bay
marked "Marfak Lubrication," said goodbye
to my chicks, told them they were going

for a ride in Frank's truck, told them
they were going someplace nice, someplace
in the country. When I got back in the car,

my mother was crying. She was looking
across the street, as she spoke softly,
said how eight years back, when I was a toddler,

she'd stopped at Frank's for gas after the funeral,
said she knew her mother's body was in a coffin
in the black Cadillac hearse right over there

under that porte-cochère, all gassed up
and waiting for the entourage that would
snake itself to a cemetery in farmland up north.

Light Time in Winter

Daylight on the playhouse and jungle gym
        enfolds the children safely, and they sense it
    everywhere—in holes and deep-rut tree bark.
Even when light reduces as dusk comes on, day is still their friend.
    The memory is there for them
        like a mother's lingering cologne
when she's not at home.

She's on her way. It's snowing,
        and she's turned the iced wipers on for transparency,
    low beams for guidance in near-sleet.
The car's heat hesitates, and tires skid, a sly crab, on the road back.
    The children lie down in the yard, fan their arms and legs,
etch crescents in the snow before night.

A Voice from the Grave in Coming-On Winter

I am being dowsed deep down
in this cold obscurity.

Is there someone in the light-time
looking for my history,

for mold that might have bloomed
on my skin, when all else—

except wind and dowser—
lie lifeless above ground?

I am safe, and creatures beside me smile
in their sleep for not being found,

which is the miracle of cold.
This sunken place drips on slightly warmer days,

and I can smell what gives me hope:
roots alive, rhizomes, bulbs, and tubers,

tightly wadded leaves, flowerets
waiting cool but not freezing dead.

Artist's Blue Hour, Oslo

for David Sandum

I've seen the photo you took yesterday
at sundown, the all-blue of your street.

You're on your way to a place,
but where? The store? The stube? The studio?

Blue needs supply. Needs eye.
Blue needs easel. Needs brush. Needs nod.

Needs song like "When you're down
and troubled." Gesture annuls crisp air

the way clouds turn sun blue over blue
over sapphire on snow. That's when

"you need a helping hand"—at the blue hour,
the down-and-troubled hour

when winter is at its bluest
and nothing soothes your red-chapped lips.

Sign: Chemotherapy Waste Must Be Incinerated

During chemo, pages turn
and go nowhere. Plots do not unfold.

Characters are ignored, unread out of worry
and confusion. Even boredom is wasted.

Better to be bored in a library
or at the mercy of a person in a pulpit

who doesn't really believe it, but says so
for your sake, since faith is your last hope.

No, it's your second to last, because an I-V
is going to fix you. Of course, it's going to

damage you, too. And no one will let on
there are no miracles. That's why evidence

that sings of ignorance must be destroyed
and incinerated, which leaves

only an insignificant pile of ash behind.

When It's Over

It stops,
but not as abruptly as that,
more like when the earworm leaves you
and you don't know it has left.

It isn't a decision,
so it's not that you don't
want it to continue,
even though you don't.

It just doesn't happen anymore.
Maybe sometimes you get a familiar feeling
and you think it's coming on,
but it doesn't.

Well, maybe something does,
but not the way you know it can.

4 Innocence & Guilt

Rage, ocean : foam, oppressions,
We stand, and these children follow and all will yet be well.

from Muriel Rukeyser, "Child and Mother" in *Theory of Flight*

In the Green Room before the Concert

Most of us
are already here,
waiting to go on.
Frank came early.
Blue blazer.
Broad-shouldered,
heavier than
he needs to be.
His wife dead
six weeks ago.

George walks in.
Maybe shuffles
is what George does.
Tall, but stooped.
Blazer rumpled.
His wife dead
two months ago.

They haven't been here
since it happened
to either of them,
George or Frank.
We've been waiting.
We're all here now.
Together in this place.
All of us.
George walks
over to Frank.
Each puts arms
around the other.

Over-Abundance

*remembering the woman who said, "I've been on a few diets
because I can't get enough to eat on just one."*

They can't stop themselves.
Daily they take twice as much
as what will do them. And they go global—
India, Italy, China, Greece, Uganda, France,
and myriad other cuisines.
(Burmese villagers asked them,
"What do you eat that's made you so big?")
It was never rice and a few leaves.
No, not for them. They don't remember
subsistence. They need more than
twice as much, thrice maybe,
and they talk of food as if it's
a designer dress, a private jet. Food
is a swimming pool. Food is a country club,
a diamond ring, sparkly humor,
laughter at all the wrong things.
Food is arranged, photographed,
the image shared with the famished world.
They can't stop themselves.

Protective Masks in Times of Appendicitis

That was then

My mother took me to the hospital.
14 years old. A clergyman,
in a black shirt and a small square
of white at his throat, held my hand,
walking and talking beside me
as I was pushed on a gurney toward the O.R.
My god, he was praying over me.
Was I about to die?
My mother, furious, told him
to stop his foolish prayers.
But that was then—when you'd stay
in a hospital for five days
after an appendectomy, or even a baby.

This is now

Sophie's coming out of surgery.
14 years old, an appendectomy—
when hospitals are vying for space,
time, personnel and equipment
during a pandemic. People are dying,
they are about to die, they have died.
Morgues are filled with the dead.
Sophie's father, my son, is with her,
both masked—"layer after layer
of protocols," he said, her protector
in an unsafe world needing prayers.
They'll go home tomorrow.

Happiness

I believe in hopeless causes.
—Peter Edward Kassig, beheaded
by ISIL, November 2014

The pursuit of it, at least,
is the pleasure.
We have knelt and fed throats.
We have massaged muscle.
We have prayed and we have not prayed.
Prayers are hopeless. Amen. So be it.
Hello, Dad. Hello, Mom.
Salaam, Imam. Teacher and legacy.
Please, sir, I want some more [porridge].
Response is the antidote to entreaty.
We will try to forgive the drone-senders.
We will try to forgive the assassins.
Comfort will come to those
pursuing happiness outside the walls.
And to all a good night.

Sign: Coffee! You Can Sleep When You're Dead

I'm wide awake.
I'm having a double espresso
here on the sidewalk.
I'm wide awake.
Slight caffeine tremor,
but my fingers
are still long and slender,
not gnarled or shaking too badly.
Yes, some acidity in my throat.
Otherwise, I'd ask for a kiss.
The barista maybe?
Or you, sitting across from me?
Besame mucho, you at your tablet.
I'm not dead yet.
I'm drinking coffee
across from you,
and the mid-morning sun
is hitting you. I remember
the touch of morning sun.
Shadow follows like a finger
the soon-to-emerge lines on your face.
I'm wide awake. I want to kiss you.
To remember young lips.
Asters are in full bloom,
slanting upward. They'll remember
to slant upward,
long after my cup is empty.

Good Times

a convolute, in which an artist talks to her alter-ego at the age of 75

You've had your good times and scars from the journey.
It is not a straight line at any age—it is a winding road.

Major shifts, thick and full, soften lines over time,
sharp defined angles. What's the rush?

Take a step back from the edge. At heart, you're keen
on adventurous stuff, ready for radiance, vines and flowers

that attract hummingbirds. Vibrant hues—it's all about color
without missing out on blue, purple, and red tones.

You know what you've got: worries about remembering.
He might not be catching the torturous repetitions.

When you're lying in bed at night or you're across
                                    from him at lunch,
get a little closer. Men have isolated themselves. Man is fragile.

You may feel tempted to taste the rainbow again, to do
what makes your heart sing. There is simply nothing else like it.

You're safe in the world. There will always be glitter,
as a finishing touch. You've had your good times.

Tenth Anniversary Forgotten, 1946

Three years after I was born,
                she was ready to give birth again.
Time to forget the war. Time to laugh. Time to get on
                with the job of making babies and money.
My father sat at the table with us three girls
                waiting for her to descend.
What could she be doing upstairs?—
                Why wasn't she dishing out our dinner?

Quiet, she's coming down now.

And that's when the bride appeared—
                in a maternity dress, and a yellowed tulle veil
gathered over her hair by combs
                festooned with silk-fertile orange-blossoms.
The groom, who had forgotten the day, had forgotten how to laugh,
                cried the most sudden tears I'd ever seen.

Infidelity

based on a found letter

This is his poem in early morning hours,
"I have been unable to sleep,
my mind's been so full of thoughts of you."

Behold his dawn-clarity aching,
which he calls love—"I am deeply passionately
in love with you"—this father of five,

this old English professor, who at long last
has succumbed to experience
what he reads and parses and teaches:

declarations of love inside letters,
slender nakednesses, assignations
that it is now his turn to write.

"I continuously see before me your dear face,
and hear your sweet voice and charming laugh,"
while his leathery wife of miscarriages

and so much raising of troublesome children
and adoration of worrisome grandchildren,
lies in their bed, coughing in her sleep.

The light is dim in his study, or it is bright
but only on his hands, pen and paper. "Darling girl,
I ask you for one thing, that you believe me."

He will leave the letter on her desk in the morning.
It is a masterpiece. And he is ready to cry out,
"My whole being yearns to be with you, always."

He feels accomplished among writers.

Eve Regrets

Remembering Miss Otis, with thanks to Cole Porter

I regret I'm unable to lunch today, Adam.
I'm sorry. I can't get out of bed.
I'm feeling low as a crawler, perhaps just guilty
of something too complicated to understand.

No, I'll not be at your table today, Adam,
no matter what the sandwich is. Or the soup.
Or is it rib day? I'm sorry. I know you love vegetables,
but I'll be sleeping in today, Adam.

Sometimes I think I *am* sleep, if not a rotor in the fan
above my head. My fever gains in circles, eddies
like the kind that come with rum and Coke
and Chianti straw bottles from the sixties.

You're still on my refrigerator door, Adam.
Yellowed memories, but tears don't come anymore.
At times I lift up my head—a lovely head,
as you yourself said in a moment of embarrassed love,

but a head and face flushed to apple-red,
enough to say I regret I'm unable to lunch today.

Jealousy

She's jealous
of his arthritis.
It loves him so much
he doesn't have time for her.
It demands that he rub his knees,
that he smother them in ice,
that he apply luscious heat,
take silken-dreamy pills.
She's jealous of his limp.
It forces him to sit
and to lie down with it.
It loves him so much
he doesn't walk with her.
Or hold her hand.
Sometimes on a sidewalk,
he slides his arm into hers,
but that's for balance.
That's how he comforts,
satisfies his limp,
his bone-on-bone.
She's jealous of his pain.
It's so insistent
in its love for him.

Olly Olly In Free

Playing kick-the-can

A fearless liberator sneaks up on whoever's *it*
and kicks the can that we always placed

on a ground-level tree stump. Anyone caught is free
to go and hide again. Like all cycles, it repeats.

Charlie was our star liberator, though we didn't know
at the time he wasn't fearless. We didn't know

that deep in our neighborhood nights, he lay in bed
listening to his father in Miriam's room.

Miriam at 16 was too beautiful and distant from us
to play kick-the-can after supper.

It was Charlie who ate fast and crossed the street
to join us every summer evening at my house,

until that one night he rushed in to liberate us,
pulled his right leg back to kick the can

and swung his foot dead-on into the ground-level tree stump.
The can continued to sit, waiting patiently for its fate.

That ended the game.

We all disappeared into the houses that held us,
while Charlie, unable to keep the sounds of night from coming,

hobbled home alone with a broken toe,
a broken spirit that we knew nothing about

until years later when Miriam died by her own hand
and Charlie told his story, blaming himself for not freeing her.

The can eventually turned up rusted and dented
under a spiræa hedge at the house of my childhood.

The Irony of Tuam, County Galway, 1925-1961

Today a local committee has been set up to press for a proper memorial, which would bear all the children's names.

David McKittrick, *The Independent*, June 6, 2014

Eight hundred innocents buried
anonymously behind The Home
where nuns had forgotten their faith.

All the little beings named by their "unwed mothers"
buried nameless, dead of one thing or another—
no distinction between bones and names.

Innocent babies (worthless) punished by nuns.
Innocent mothers (nobodies) punished by nuns.
Charity (name)—a word of an indifferent Church.

Creating life out of inexperience, sin.
Creating life out of violence, sin.
Creating life without permission from God, sin.

Each mother knows her child's name,
and it is Grace. Hope. Comfort. Chrystal.
Laughter. Curiosity. Sound. Vowels. Rhymes.

But the greatest of these is Irony.

Birds Keep No Borders

3 skinnys for June 23, 2019, the Rio Grande

Father and daughter drowned,
facedown,
river
separating
families
facedown,
languages,
nations,
love
facedown,
daughter and father drowned.

Birds keep no borders.
Freedom
resides
in
birdsong—
freedom
from
cages'
limiting
freedom.
No borders keep birds.

Daughter and father, sing.
Fly
across
border-
rivers.
Fly
your
song
home.

Fly.
Sing, father and daughter.

Amuse Bouche, the Ortolan

The felony is that they trap the songbird in Aquitaine.
They fatten it, in a dark box, on millet, drown it in Armagnac.
The felony is that they sell it for €150 to a restaurant.

The little rose-breasted bunting—mouthful of tune—
is losing its flock, bouche by bouche.
The plucked and footless morsel roasts for eight minutes

in a ramekin, goes whole into the mouth
but not without the ritual of the napkin held
so that delicious vapors steam into the gourmand's nostrils,

and the mess of gluttony—sizzling fat and crisp droppings—
is shielded from the eyes of the All-Knowing,
who would never forgive the felony of eating song.

Fire of London, September 2-6, 1666

". . . for all that fire, the traditional death toll reported
is extraordinarily low: just six verified deaths."
                    —Rose Eveleth, smithsonian.com, March 4, 2014

There's a reason for those three sixes
in 1666. The devil played his tricks
that year over those infernal days.

He cremated human after human
(there were many hundreds more than six),
and he made sure that no one cared

who they were, being merely
of the poor and the middle class.
The devil made them live nameless

and die nameless and without a resting place.
He made sure no one cared, and the nobles
rejoiced that no one to speak of had died.

Kingdom of Blood

for Irom Sharmila Chanu,
in memory of Nangeli, who defied the breast tax

Nangeli shawled her breasts with cloth
when she went out into the street.
The king sent the tax collector
to make her pay for daring to impersonate
a high-caste woman with covered breasts.

The king does not pay a tax.
The king makes the rules. The rules force
the poor to pay tax. The rules allow
soldiers to kill. The king says the soldiers
can kill whomever they suspect.

Sharmila stops eating to stop the killing,
but the king says she's killing only herself
and the kingdom has rules against that.
The king puts a tube down her throat
to prevent internal bleeding from starvation.

In the street Nangeli dropped the cloth
and with a knife cut off each breast.
Blood flowed out from her and she died.
Like every woman who bleeds, she knew
that her wounds would heal.

Torture One

The person who finds it easy
to use electric shock on a penis,

to hang a human being by the arms,
to beat the bottom of a woman's feet,

to sic a dog on an ankle,
to pour water over a face—

to whom was this person born?
Who fed this person from her own breast?

Who taught this person to hurt another creature?
What voices did this person hear in the cradle?

Torture Two

The Sheik [was] caught on camera allowing his horse to be beaten by a groom.—Daily Mail, June 16, 2014

You love to beat flesh.
You love to watch
someone beat flesh.

Horse's flesh.
A horse. A horse.
A creature for your bidding.

A horse. A horse.
English countryside
before the first chukker.

To beat flesh brings you
into the pleasure of kings.
Money buys.

A horse, a groom.
Two creatures for your bidding.

Conversation

after a visit to a medieval torture exhibit

What good is torture?
> *None. It serves no truth.*

What if torture does serve truth?
> *Truth doesn't show in blood.*

What if the torture is inadvertent?
> *There's no such thing.*

What if it's threatened?
> *That's torture.*

What if there's no trace of torture?
> *There's always a trace.*

What about getting beaten on the soles of your feet?
> *No trace is still a scar.*

What if the cause is over?
> *A torturer never loses the taste for hurting.*

Will you hold my hand?
> *Yes. As long as you want me to.*

Sign: Please Use Other Door to Enter⟶

An arrow points toward something else,
but you can't be sure there's another door.

You want to use a forbidden one.
Entering is all that's left.

Knobs go both ways.
Doors push, doors pull,

if you can get to them. Even a buzzer
is a miracle for calling out,

but there's no light to speak of
when a barrier fills transparency,

and iron bars separate you
from those who have already entered.

Inside, the door closes. Torture,
a beating on the soles, makes exit impossible.

Pre-PTSD

They laugh and sit
against the insides of jets
and helicopters and other spaces.

They obey orders like good kids,
packs on their backs
and boots the color of desert.

They laugh and smoke cigarettes
and maryjane if they can get it.
They laugh and make friends.

They laugh and smoke
and look at pictures
before the mortar round

puts them in recovery
but for one week only
when they're out again

and getting in the way
of mortar rounds.
They laugh and smoke.

       *   *   *   *

And then they're out for good.
They drink with buddies,
and they laugh and smoke,

free to wander in the streets,
to get addicted
to meth among the tweakers.

Solitary

Solitary breathes mold that rubs off the walls.
Solitary bleeds hours into years. Solitary
echoes in an 8-by-6 for 23 hours a day.

Solitary conspires. You look behind
your back. Crickets that sing.
They crawl on you at night.

Decades, and more months lie ahead
with Solitary your daily companion. Solitary
will not be injected with anything lethal.

No gurney for Solitary. Solitary gets no last supper.
Fajitas, triple-meat bacon cheeseburgers, pizzas,
chicken fried steaks, okra, ice cream with peanuts.

Irony makes you laugh. You like the feel of
laughter in your gut. Solitary laughs at you.
You slide down into a corner, giggle, cry,

roar, tremble before Solitary, Almighty Solitary,
which is nothing, nobody, neither one nor the other,
and never and never and never.

Sign: No Parking At Any Time

I emerged from a womb
drugged with sodium pentothal.
Everything in slow motion:
slap, cry, fingers.
One. Five. Ten.
In no time, slow quickens.
I'm breathing
and speeding on my own road.
Twenty-five at first. Fifty-five.
Ninety. Ninety-five.
A hundred and ten—
to get there as fast as possible.
At any time, forgive my memories.
There are so many now.
I leave the rules to you.
I know I can't stay here

Notes
Anne Harding Woodworth

Page 15. A one-act, one-woman play of "Hannah Alive," in which I kept the poetry presented here, was performed in a staged reading by actor Kimberly Schraf in the Washington, D.C., metropolitan area at the Nora School Poetry Series, October 2015. The play was a finalist in the 2016 Adirondack Shakespeare Company's Dramatic Writing Competition in the One-Act category and had a reading in Essex, New York.

Page 43. "Daisy Chain": I had a high school classmate, who had a big role in student government. She was everyone's friend, kind and generous. One of the most enjoyable school outings was to pick daisies for the daisy chain that 11th-graders carried at commencement. Some years after high school this friend was diagnosed with mental illness. R.I.P.

Pages 48-50. "The Sig Poems": These poems are based on correspondence received by a lawyer from his high school friend, Sig, who after a few years as a student at Harvard was diagnosed with schizophrenia, which led to a life of wandering, extreme paranoia, institutionalization, and incarceration resulting from confrontations with the police.

Page 51. "A Mental Health Hospital Closes": I read an article about a mental health hospital closing in Iowa. Many such hospitals were built in the heyday of "insane asylums" (late 19th century) along the lines of the Kirkbride Plan, which was called "bat-wing" style.

Page 55: "By Reason of Insanity": ". . . left the grounds of the D.C. psychiatric hospital . . ." (*Washington Post*, May 4, 2014).

Page 60: "Swing Time": "A woman was found . . . pushing her dead three-year-old son on a swing." (*Washington Post*, May 22, 2015).

Page 63. "The Heel Stone at Stonehenge":
http://www.stonesofstonehenge.org.uk.

Page 64. The Collection de l'Art Brut is a museum in Lausanne, Switzerland, that specializes in outlier art.

Page 65. "Horse Dress, 1939": I saw the actual Horse Dress on display at the American Visionary Art Museum, Baltimore, MD.

Page 69: "Insecure in an Age of Synthesis" was created from sundry words and phrases contained in *Cosmopolitan*, November 2017. It is what I call "a convolute," a term I have borrowed from the German philosopher Walter Benjamin, whose compilation of disparate lines, photos, ads, texts, etc. in the 1930s make up his *konvolute*. Other convolutes appear on pp. 73 and 114.

Pages 70-72. "Echo of the Frogs": Withaney here is my alter-ego, created when I was a child to remind others that Anne is spelled with an e. I must confess that I used to say that Withaney was a family name. ". . . *be grateful to the mirror . . .*" Samuel Butler.

Page 73. "Water on the Moon": This convolute (see note for page 69) was created from sundry words and phrases contained in *The New York Times*, the *BBC*, and a piece suggesting water on the moon at *space.com*, June 23-24, 2017.

Page 80. "Sign: Fragile Roof." I have included five "sign" poems in this collection. I take photographs of signs that are evocative of metaphor, irony, humor, ignorance, etc. A photo becomes the actual title of the poem, which would have been prohibitive in this collection. Besides "Fragile Roof," the other four are: "Chemotherapy Waste Must Be Incinerated" (p. 105), "Coffee! You Can Sleep When You're Dead" (p. 113), "Please Use Other Door to Enter→" (p. 131), and "No Parking At Any Time" (p. 134).

Page 84. "The Miniaturist, 1828" is based on the life of Sarah

Goodrich (1788-1853), who had an affair with Daniel Webster and painted for him what today might be called a sext.

Page 85. "Quiet Air": "Come home, wind, he kept crying and crying" with thanks to Wallace Stevens, "Pieces."

Page 86. "Winter Night, a Lullaby," was set to music in three parts by Bundy H. Boit for an *a capella* sextet. I recorded it with some friends whom I have known through The City Choir of Washington. Chosen by *Flock Literary Journal* along with eleven other lullabys, the recording can be heard here at EAT. http://www.eatwords.net/2018/12/

Pages 89-90. "Fire in the Pale Green Bedroom" came out of a frightening experience when our dear friend across the hall from us found her bedroom on fire early on a December morning, 2019. Her apartment was destroyed.

Pages 91-92. "Sleeplessness": "I hear the humming of my blood" is from Ruben Dario's "Nocturne."

Page 97. "Whitman's Last Words": Krieg, Joann P. "Letters from Warry." *Walt Whitman Quarterly Review* 11 (Spring 1994), 163-173. https://doi.org/10.13008/2153-3695.1419

Page 102. "Light Time in Winter" with thanks to Wallace Stevens, "The Prejudice Against the Past."

Page 103. "A Voice from the Grave in Coming-On Winter" is based on my poem, "Wintering," which appeared in my chapbook *Up from the Root Cellar*, Cervena Barva Press, 2007. Here it takes on a slightly different tone.

Page 110. "Over-Abundance" was originally a sign poem, but I changed the title and incorporated what was on the sign into an epigraph.

Page 114. "Good Times": a convolute (see note for page 69) created from sundry words and phrases contained in *Cosmopolitan*, June 2018.

Page 123. "Birds Keep No Borders" is in the form of a skinny. The skinny, invented by poet Truth Thomas, consists of eleven lines, all but first and last lines being a single word, with specific repetition.

Page 132: "Pre-PTSD": with thanks to Richard Johnson for his sketches in the *Washington Post*, July 13, 2014.

Page 133. "Solitary": This poem looks at solitary confinement, coming out of a story about a trio of murderers, one of whom was in solitary, while one of his two accomplices was on death row and the other was executed by lethal injection.

I'd like to take this opportunity to thank Stanley Palombo for his reading of *Trouble* in manuscript and for suggesting that "Hannah Alive" go first.

CPSIA information can be obtained
at www.ICGtesting.com
Printed in the USA
LVHW011956081220
673650LV00004B/484

9 781625 493613